Lerik

the Free Shipping Unicorn

by J. Finley Hendricks

Lerik the Free Shipping Unicorn

Copyright © 2017 by J. Finley Hendricks

ISBN-13: 978-0998675305

alauda creative

For those who provided inspiration and commiseration during the creation of this book.

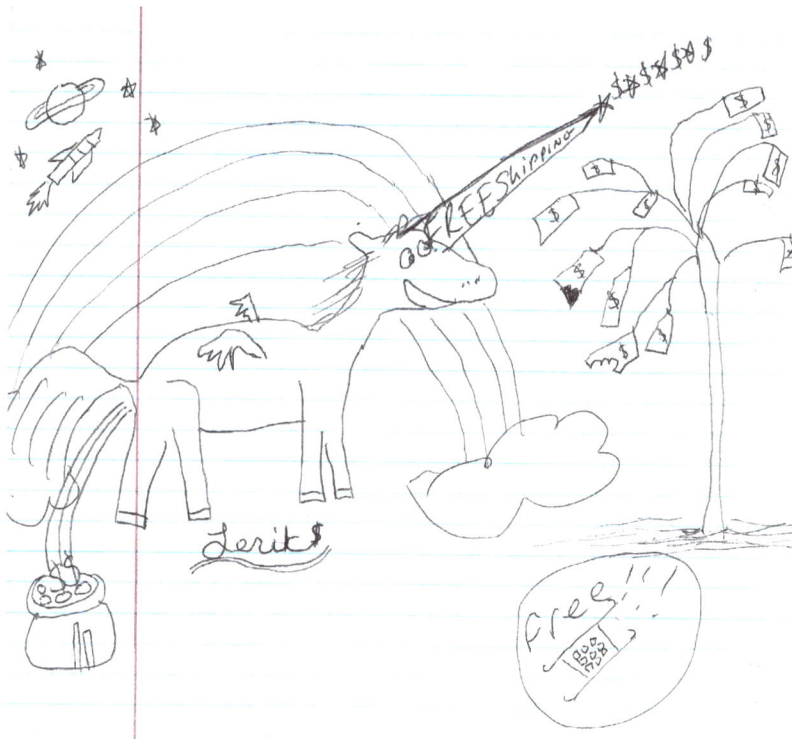

The Beginning

There once was a businessman with a pungent smell,
A strong outer glow, and a desire to sell.
He got a taste for the fruit of the money tree,
Then met an enchanted puma named Furr Rawrrree.

Furr Rawrrree told him tales of sea and sand,
Yachts and sunshine, and "your own private island."
"That sounds great," said the man with a wide-eyed stare,
"But I have something to take care of before I go there..."

"In order to leave but still have some clout,"
Furr Rawrrree replied, "...just sell out."
So sell out he did, and off they flew,
Carrying along a bag of money or two.

His business was put into some slick, slimy fingers
Full of promises, but the greed of the game still lingered.
"Squeeze out every cent!" "How will we do that?"
There was an unusual and magical trick in their hat...

From the depths of marketing's shallows was born
Lerik the Free Shipping Unicorn!

Marketing Tactics

Lerik's marketing prowess was polished and bold,
As if he could take dirt and turn it to gold.
He could spin numbers like he was spinning plates,
Create the most amazing sales with the most amazing rates.

10% OFF!

SALE

Value propositions were born and bred
With genius design ideas like "make it red."
'Make it bigger and brighter! Make it look fast!
Buy this now! This sale won't last!!!"

BUY THIS!!!!!

"For a limited time only - don't miss this deal!
In stock! Ships today! This bargain's a steal!!!"
On and on and on, the ploys wouldn't stop.
One way or another, customers would shop.

Lerik couldn't stop with the markety squawking.
He couldn't get enough and then started stalking.
Do you exist online? Lerik will find you there.
Did you buy something? You need more. Buyer beware.

Money trees taste sweet, but they tend to disrupt
With an insatiable hunger that slowly corrupts...

Psychological Torture

Lerik lost control of his money-lust desire,
Climbing over others to make himself higher.
He'd be your friend one minute, pat you on the back,
Then slowly stick the knife in with a subtle attack.

Lerik put on so many faces, he grew two more heads,
Arguing with himself until they all turned bright red.
But one thing they could agree on, despite the fights,
Was to keep all the peon workers square in their sights.

One head had the temper of a two-year old child,
Make you work till you bleed, but still get all riled.
The next would say, "great job!" with a helping of phony,
Then set you up to fail and hire his cronies.

The third acted like there was nothing he couldn't do,
But was a back-stabbing jerk, just like the other two.
The three together were a sad but strong force
That set the company on a greedy and downward course.

It happened more like a slow boil than a violent eruption,
But the once-ok place turned into a deceptive realm of corruption.

The Battle/Fleeing

Lerik's constant scheming became hard to take,
Starting a battle, of sorts, between real and fake.
Like a narwhal and unicorn going head to head:
A glittery myth clashing with grey, and some spirits gone dead.

Some tried to make things work; they gave it their best.
But it wasn't ever good enough – they could get no rest,
Just an earful of cursing, manipulation, and lies.
It was no wonder they all started dropping like flies.

Lerik's assault of fakeness was easy to see through.
The remaining weren't dumb, and some could still be true.
But he was still a bully, deliberate with whom he sparred,
Not realizing how tough the little ones are.

Sort of pointless, this battle, horn to tusk.
It left everyone, on both sides, like a dry empty husk.
The peon narwhals, disaffected and unsure of their role,
And exploitative Lerik with a head like a hole.

Lerik thought he was invincible, that everyone was his prey.
He was too proud to see, in and out, he was beginning to decay...

Decay

Lerik's mesmerizing sparkle had become rather faded.
Everyone around him was now unimpressed and jaded.
Bored to tears, with no reason to trust,
They watched Lerik's horns begin to rust.

Little by little, he started to break down.
His saccharin smile turned into a frown.
He shot himself in the foot till it was a bloody stump.
His once flowing mane was a nasty snarled clump.

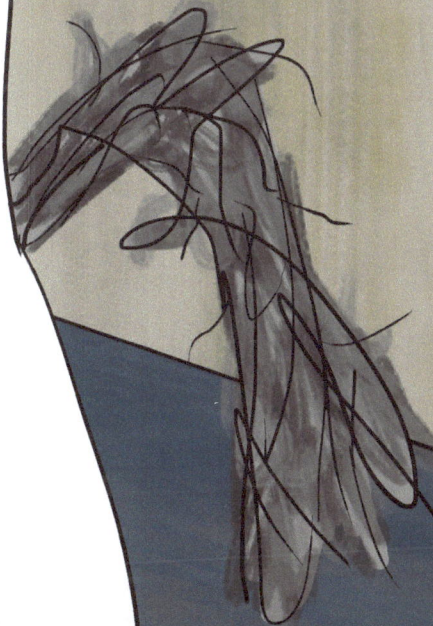

After so much time scratching backs and filling pockets,
Lerik's eyes, the windows to his "soul," became dry empty sockets.
From stuffing his gullet with whatever he could contrive,
Stage 4 Avarice began to eat him alive.

If Lerik had feelings, he might have been deeply sad.
But, all in all, the whole thing was quite mad.
The glitter, the rot, the build-up, the ripping –
In the end, it's not really worth the free shipping.

www.ingramcontent.com/pod-product-compliance
Lightning Source LLC
Chambersburg PA
CBHW040020050426
42452CB00002B/70

9780998675305